ESTIMATING
ECONOMIC CAPACITY

A UNIVERSITY OF
KENTUCKY STUDY

Estimating Economic Capacity

A SUMMARY OF CONCEPTUAL PROBLEMS

by

Richard E. Gift

UNIVERSITY OF KENTUCKY PRESS
Lexington, 1968

For Becky

PREFACE

In view of the variety of methods by which capacity is measured along with the differences that are found in the definition of the concept itself, it is well to state here that I conceive of capacity measurement as the estimation of probable shortrun responses by productive establishments to specific hypothetical alterations of economic conditions.

I have confined myself in this monograph to those problems that are inherent in the idea of economic capacity itself and have avoided many serious problems having to do with the measurement of capital, the measurement of output, the philosophy of measurement, and the mathematical properties of production functions.

It needs to be emphasized strongly that the purpose here is *not* to develop a new concept of capacity or a new procedure for estimating it. Rather, it is to cope with the multiplicity of concepts and measures that already exist and with the frequent failure of estimates prepared by different methods to be in agreement.

The task has been divided into four steps. The first is to show that all capacity concepts and arguments have a common structure, which consists of a list of variables that are always pertinent when assessing the economic capacity of productive equipment. The second is to show that the problems which arise in aggregating capacity estimates and in comparing capacities for different dates can be expressed in the form of a few simple generalizations. The third is to illustrate specific problems that arise in preparing and interpreting capacity estimates. The fourth is to develop a test for the logical completeness of any argument about capacity.

So that the frame of reference for the discussion will be clear, the various types of capacity measurements should be listed at this point. They are as follows:

1. Output and capital-stock data for a previous peak in production or in capital outlay are used as the frame of reference.

   (*a*) Capacity is measured by peak-forward extrapolation of output (sometimes with the presumption that the peak output corresponds to the minimum average cost point) either from a point of peak-attainment or from a point at which a decision was made to expand fixed capital.

   (*b*) A capital-output ratio is measured at a previous peak in output or capital outlays, and capacity is computed for each following period by "plugging in" the then current capital stock (as actually measured or as estimated by peak-forward extrapolation on the basis of (1) capital stock in the reference period, (2) depreciation rates, and (3) records on net increases of capital stock since the reference period).

   (*c*) Capital outlays are measured and simply assumed to reflect the behavior of capacity.

2. The composite response to direct inquiry on capacity by mail questionnaires is the frame of reference.

(a) The capacity survey is open-ended.

(b) The survey questionnaire specifies a concept of capacity.

(c) The questionnaire does not specify a concept of capacity but does ask pointed questions that make it possible for the surveyor to apply a definite concept which he has in mind.

(d) The survey seeks engineers' estimates of installed capacity or the original ratings of machines in each plant's equipment.

3. A production function containing empirical coefficients is used together with data on the current sizes of the stocks of productive inputs to estimate capacity for a domain of firms for which the production function used is believed to be relevant. Such a production function may be derived either from engineering estimates or from data on actual historical performance.

4. Capacity is regarded as an output that is consistent with some input-output table or with some system of linear or nonlinear constraints, expressed mathematically.

Substantial financial assistance was given to this project by Duke University in the form of a Ford Foundation Workshop Grant and a Summer Scholarship, and by Davidson College in the form of two grants from the Faculty Committee on Research and Summer Study. Dr. Frank A. Hanna, professor of economics at Duke University, has given substantial and constructive criticism to my work. To all these I wish to express my gratitude.

Lexington, Kentucky   R.E.G.
January 2, 1968

CONTENTS

TABLES

1

THE DETERMINANTS
OF ECONOMIC CAPACITY

$\mathcal{J}_T$ *IS* widely believed by economists and others that many economic and political events are deeply affected by the relationship between actual and possible production. An outgrowth of this belief has been the development of a number of published statistical series on economic capacity. In attempting to prepare and interpret capacity estimates, it is helpful to have a model that defines and shows what determines capacity and which does so for any level of aggregation of establishments or of products. Within such a framework the true differences between alternative concepts can be found, and possible reasons for differences between independently prepared estimates can be suggested.

The shortrun constraints upon an establishment's output expansion are the amount of fixed capital, its adaptability, and its productivity; the prices, qualities, and availabilities of other inputs; the shortrun possibilities for outright factor substitution and equipment conversion; the firm's desired financial position and the availability and cost of short-term credit; expected output prices, the expected level of new and unfilled orders, and the minimum tolerable quality of the output; and the de facto goals of the firm, as they relate to shortrun profit maximization.

There are several ways in which fixed plant and equipment may become inadaptable as production increases. Floorspace may become inadequate in such a way that additional employees would merely hamper operations. The equipment may be sufficiently indivisible so that there is simply nothing for additional employees to do, even though they may not hinder the work. Even if there is adequate floorspace and equipment, it may be impossible to teach new employees the necessary skills within the length of time required to carry out successfully a quick expansion of output. Even if additional workers can be employed, trained, assigned to usable equipment, and given enough space for orderly and safe operations, it still may not be possible to take full advantage of such opportunities if the managerial and supervisory personnel are not sufficient in number to supervise the work effectively. Furthermore, a bottleneck at some particular stage in the chain of operations may be caused either by the fact that the equipment at this stage is less flexible than at other stages, or by the fact that there is a shortage of the special kind of labor or materials needed at this stage, or both. A bottleneck of this kind can occur not only at an intermediate stage but also at the beginning or end of the sequence of operations. A firm may be unable to obtain materials that, if available, could be used efficiently; or it may find that transportation and storage facilities are inadequate, so that it is unable to divest itself of its output at a sufficient rate to avoid damage due to improper storage.

Suppose that a firm's operations consist of three production stages (A, B, and C) other than the receiving and shipping departments and that the fixed equipment in Department B is the most inadaptable in the entire plant. If this is the case, then the firm's output is said to be constrained by Department B, regardless of what Department A can send on to B or of what C can do with anything B can forward to it. Similarly, if no more labor of the kind needed in Department A can be obtained in the short run, then the firm's output cannot exceed its current output, unless some form of outright factor substitution is possible. Furthermore, suppose that some raw material needed at stage C is being rationed by the government. In this case, output is constrained by this particular bottleneck, regardless of how much intermediate output Department B could pour into C. Again, this conclusion must be modified in any situation where outright factor substitution is possible in the short run, and, furthermore, such bottlenecks as these sometimes exist only with reference to a minimal standard of quality for the final output.

Although the significance of any specific bottleneck in an establishment's operations is diminished if there is some other way in which the particular function can be performed, in view of the amount of time available for adjustment, many establishments do not face significant possibilities for outright substitution in the short run, for two reasons.[1] First, this kind of factor substitution usually implies a change of process, even if merely on a small scale, and virtually every productive process requires some fixed capital. While an establishment's fixed capital may be quite adapt-

[1] Whenever factor proportions are varied by employing a greater quantity of a variable input, then factor substitution is taking place by definition. However, at this point we are concerned only with outright factor substitution, that is, only with those cases in which a variable input assumes some new function as output expands, as when newly employed workers begin to do work by hand which is ordinarily done by machine.

able to varying numbers of man-hours under a use of the process for which the capital equipment was intended, it is unlikely that such equipment would be appropriate for a different process. (It could happen, of course, that part of the stock of fixed capital is a pool of equipment or tools designed for an alternate process kept under wraps for just such a contingency.) Second, since outright factor substitution may involve using poorly trained workers or a relatively labor-intensive method, or both, or may require drawing into use a line of obsolete equipment, the relative inefficiency of the method to be substituted would often make its cost prohibitive. Exceptions to this could arise in cases where alternative parts, materials, fuels, or storage methods can easily be substituted for each other or in industries where some of the mechanical facilities are sufficiently convertible so that they can be transferred readily from one use to another (as, for example, in sheet metal work). But, in general, the ability to substitute is low in the short run.

Some industrial operations do not allow a variation of shift arrangements as a means of increasing output, and, in some of these cases, overtime work is either useless or too costly. The stock of fixed capital is thus a much more rigid constraint in an industry where multiple shift operations are compulsory (as in chemical distillation) than where they are optional (as in spinning and printing). In industries of the latter type, the constraining elements are the added labor costs to be incurred on the production line during extra hours of operation and the associated increases in the costs experienced for handling, servicing, cleaning, and repair.

The ability of a firm to use whatever adaptability may be possessed by its fixed plant and equipment is limited by the prices of the variable inputs and by the depreciation charges for the fixed inputs. During an expansion of output the additional costs will consist of the new employment costs incurred in hiring or buying extra units of the variable

4

inputs and of any increases in depreciation charges that may be judged desirable or necessary in view of the more intense utilization of the fixed plant and equipment. The amount of new outlay required for these purposes as output expands is just as surely a constraint as is the degree of inadaptability of the fixed capital goods. Aside from the purely financial constraints upon the amount of this outlay, it is governed by the prices of the variable factors of production and by other increases in costs that are associated with the employment of increased flows of the variable-input services. This is the role of a price of a variable input (or of a depreciation charge) in constraining an output expansion. The influence of such a price on shortrun decision-making is the same regardless of whether the price is set by a competitive market, by collective bargaining, by a monopolistic or quasi-monopolistic supplier, or by the administrators of a government cost-control program, except whenever a particular method of factor pricing has some special effect upon the expectations or morale of workers or managers, or upon the flexibility of managerial policies.

A projected shortrun output expansion may be completely feasible in view of the adaptability and factor-cost constraints and yet not be undertaken because of a lack of adequate funds to cover the additional costs. In such a case, the marginal worker is not hired even though he is productive enough to cover his wage, his training costs, and a modest interest charge on his advance. The operating funds of a firm are limited in the short run by credit conditions in the economy, by the financial position (debt-equity ratio) of the firm, and by the firm's desire for liquidity.

Even if a firm would not violate its highest tolerable debt-equity ratio by obtaining new credit, or even if it would not sacrifice badly needed liquidity by taking on new workers, there are three additional reasons why it may not be possible to finance a shortrun expansion of output. First, credit may be both desired by the firm and available

5

at some rate of interest or discount and yet unacceptable to the firm because of the magnitude of the interest charge. Second, it is possible that the firm may not be able to obtain credit because the local banking community does not consider the firm to be within the circle of preferred borrowers under given conditions in the economy. Third, the firm's creditors may think that the firm would become, or is already, overextended, even if this opinion is not shared by the management of the firm.

Fluctuation of the circle of preferred borrowers is not likely to be a major factor in the determination of capacity. Credit is not likely to be tight during the kind of expansionary conditions that are usually hypothesized (at least implicitly) in the definition of capacity, and, in any case, major manufacturing and mining firms are likely to remain within the banking community's circle of preferred borrowers under all conditions except perhaps that of a severe depression.

With a condition of general expansion in the economic system, there are further reasons why financial constraints are not likely to be as significant as one might at first expect. During the part of a business expansion that comes before the central bank initiates restraining policies, interest charges would not be expected to act as a widespread constraint in the production planning of business firms. Furthermore, as commodity prices rise, the opportunity cost of holding cash balances rises, and, in addition, the value of these balances declines. These circumstances would offset the tendency of a low interest charge to encourage the holding of idle balances, and, in any case, it is during a time of falling, not rising, commodity prices that a businessman is likely to have a high liquidity preference.

Some circumstances, however, could create a strong desire for liquidity which could in turn act as a constraint upon shortrun output expansion. (Each of these circumstances is more likely to have a significant effect on the behavior of a small firm than of a large one.) A firm may have unfavorable expectations about the continuation of good business conditions or about its ability to resist wage increases. Or, in the process of planning an expansion of its plant facilities, it may wish to retain and even accumulate liquid assets as working capital and as an exhibit for the improvement of its standing with the banking community. Furthermore, where the management wishes to prevent a dilution of control (as in some family-dominated enterprises), there may be a generalized unwillingness to borrow.

In general, then, the determination of capacity requires a description of the policy milieu in the economy with regard to credit conditions. This will include a mention of a representative interest rate on short-term credit. (Presumably, a firm would not issue long-term bonds or new corporate stocks in order to finance a shortrun expansion, and it would be difficult in any case to obtain new equity capital during a short adjustment period because of Securities and Exchange Commission regulations and the administrative lags associated with stock issue.) The interest rates in a policy milieu can be expected to affect both a firm's demand for loanable funds (and its ability to get them if the attitudes of bankers are affected by a tendency to treat the discount rate as a signal of future conditions and government policies) and also its desired asset-liability structure.

The interacting adjustments of credit flows and liquidity needs on the part of business firms during a general expansion of activity in the economic system are such that it seems reasonable to suppose that, if the interest rates are low in an expansion, then the adjustments that would take place would be favorable to the seeking of loanable funds and adverse to the holding of idle balances. Even though a lower interest charge has the effect of reducing the penalty on holding idle balances, rising prices and optimistic expectations would strongly tempt firms to use what liquid capital they have and to obtain more on credit. Even if it is believed, because of a large amount of slack in the system,

7

that the next business expansion will be characterized by stable prices and stable or gently rising interest rates, the credit factor will ordinarily become a constraining factor only after other constraints have also begun to operate.

The estimation of a reasonable potential output requires the assumption that under plausible future business conditions the level of demand would be sufficient to absorb that output. The consideration of demand conditions must, of course, take into account outlay by public authorities along with the demand of private buyers.

The information (or "signals") on demand conditions which the firm uses in its production planning only has significance when viewed in terms of the de facto aspirations for the firm which are held by its decision-makers (just as was the case with credit conditions). A firm in which profits tend to be maximized in the short run will behave differently from a firm that is attempting to maximize something else, say, market share.

In short, capacity output has its meaning only within the context of a signal (such as a change in the frequency of orders or a change in price) or signals for changes in private and public demand; and the signal itself has significance only within the context of the de facto goals of the firm. Decisions on the level of employment and production arise from the targets and aspirations of plant managers, as modified by the attitudes of creditors, stockholders, employees, and union leaders.

The revenue and cost situation considered in capacity estimation is based upon input and output prices associated with a condition of high activity in the economy, and it is the *comparative* relationships of such prices that crucially affect capacity. (These relationships are affected at all times by the magnitude of taxation on sales, property, and income, and by the prevailing method of allocating joint costs.) In short, the economic capacity of an industry can be affected by price changes alone.

Capacity is greater to the degree that the prices of the

8

variable inputs do not tend to increase as output expands. That is, an estimate of capacity should be lower (or higher) than would otherwise be the case if prices (including wages) in the markets for the variable inputs cannot be expected to remain constant (and thus leave undisturbed the average total cost curve[2]) as output increases in the short run.

The existence of 100 percent utilization depends upon the conformity of actual demand conditions to those that are assumed to be required to stimulate capacity-level production in the preparation of the capacity estimate. The capacity of an establishment with given fixed plant and equipment is relative to the date upon which an expansion to capacity would be supposed to begin, to the price and wage structure associated with such an expansion, to the product or group of products under consideration, and to the motives of the establishment's high-level managers.

One hundred percent utilization, then, is simply human behavior that fulfills a set of conditions. The significance of any one element, say plant size, as a constraint depends upon a number of other considerations. Plant size may not be a constraint if there is a materials bottleneck or a low level of demand. *Something* always constrains output; there is always a complete set of *empirical* magnitudes for the variables in the constraint list. Capacity estimation is concerned with the role of such things as plant size as constraints under *hypothetical* circumstances where lack of demand is usually assumed *not* to be an active constraint. Capacity estimation is concerned with what would happen in the short run if demand conditions suddenly became more favorable.

The magnitude of a utilization percentage for a particular date or period will vary, depending upon which of

[2] Hickman has properly noted that "changes in efficiency—in cost per unit of output—as output is varied along a *given* cost function do not affect capacity." Bert Hickman, "Capacity, Capacity Utilization, and the Acceleration Principle," in National Bureau of Economic Research, *Problems of Capital Formation* (Princeton: Princeton University Press, 1957), 421.

9

four possible procedures is followed. The alternatives are (1) to value both actual output and capacity output at the actual price(s) existing at the date or in the period to which the estimate applies, (2) to value actual output at actual price(s) and capacity output at the hypothetical price(s) which is (are) supposed to be that (those) which will be associated with the next business expansion after the date or period to which the estimate refers, (3) to value both actual output and capacity output at the hypothetical price(s), or (4) to value actual output at the hypothetical price(s) and capacity output at the actual price(s). The first alternative is the most convenient. The second and third are meaningful, but are unworkable whenever any substantial amount of aggregation over products is involved. The fourth is absurd.

As already shown, a capacity estimate for any establishment or group of establishments possesses a fundamental relativity. This relativity can be well illustrated by considering the Eastern Kentucky coalfields.

Any capacity estimate presupposes the concurrence with capacity-level production of a level of demand adequate to clear the estimated capacity output from the market. This implies either the assumption that the level of aggregate demand for goods and services in the economy at large would be such as to produce robust conditions in the market for the grade of coal that is mined in Eastern Kentucky or that, regardless of conditions in the economy at large, the private and public demand in this particular market would be high. This makes it clear that, with either of these assumptions, a capacity estimate is related essentially to an assumed business-cycle state or public-policy environment, or both. It is related to the public-policy situation because monetary policy and public outlays are clearly ingredients in aggregate demand. The exact nature of the public-policy environment is crucial, because if government contracts for coal delivery are to involve cost-plus agreements or subsidization (either of which might well be the case in a national emergency), then the capacity estimate should be larger than otherwise would be the case. This is because such policies would permit the carrying out of marginal operations involving overtime charges, increased maintenance costs, obsolete equipment and currently nonoptimal methods, and inferior veins. (The policy environment is also relevant insofar as it affects the cost structure of the coal industry by way of laws pertaining to reforestation, minimum wage, and collective bargaining.)

Whenever product differentiation exists, as in the coal industry, the assumptions about necessary demand conditions which are implicit in a capacity estimate are even more intricate than those mentioned above. The demand for coal is really a structure of demands for various grades of coal (which are only *partially* substitutes for one another) for which there is a structure of prices. In making an estimate for a particular coalfield, like Eastern Kentucky, one is assuming a certain hypothetical level of necessary demand for the grade of coal mined and processed in that field. Technical changes in the economy, external to the coal industry, can change the structure of demands for the various grades of coal. This means that a capacity estimate for a particular field could be too high simply because the hypothetical demand for that grade of coal cannot reasonably be supposed to be forthcoming during any future expansion of production in the industry at large in view of technological changes in coal usage. That is to say, changes in the structure *or* level of demand for the output of the coal industry at large can occur which are of an adverse nature for a particular field. Such adverse changes can make a portion of the physical facilities and labor supply in that field irrelevant for the estimation of capacity. As far as the Eastern Kentucky field is concerned, adverse structural changes have developed for this relatively expensive grade of coal.

A capacity estimate is also based on the assumption that there will be a continuation of some given technology in the industry under consideration. For even with an assumed hypothetical demand (which might in some cases happen to be also the actual current level of demand), the relevance of a particular capital equipment and labor combination for capacity estimation depends upon the efficiency (in view of the assumed level of demand) of this combination in relation to other combinations in the industry. For example, the answer to the question of whether the technically possible output of a particular truck mine or pony mine is to be included in an industrywide or fieldwide coal-capacity estimate has been profoundly affected by the emergence of strip mining and auger mining and by innovations in underground mining.

The intricacy of the role of demand (and its signals: output price and the level of new and unfilled orders) and technology in a capacity estimate goes still deeper. When the output of an industry has substitutes, the firms in the industry compete not only with each other but also with firms in other industries. This means that technological changes largely external to the bulk of the production operation can change entirely the significance of equipment and workers, as far as capacity estimation is concerned, with no visible change in said equipment and workers. Technological improvements in competing industries adversely affect true economic capacity in the coal industry, and improvement in transportation methods (such as the development of liquid shipping) in the coal industry favorably affect its economic capacity. Similarly, the discovery of new ways of using coal can affect favorably the true economic capacity.

The significance of a given facility for a capacity estimate is also related to cost conditions, especially the labor market. This point is clearly illustrated in Eastern Kentucky, where the presence of unemployed workers who are willing and able to work at less than the union wage has permitted the reopening of previously closed truck mines which had been forced to shut down because of competition from highly mechanized mines.

12

Hickman regards capacity as that rate of production at which the management would become dissatisfied with the amount of its fixed plant and equipment.[3] He holds that this output corresponds to the point of minimum average costs.[4] In order for a capacity estimate, which is prepared by the common (though obviously not universal) procedure of assuming that the estimate applies to demand conditions associated with cyclical peaks, to conform to Hickman's concept, two assumptions are required: First, at any time when one's estimated capacity output is actually achieved, managerial expectations about the continuation of a high level of demand must be positive (or else Hickman's *dissatisfaction* will not occur). Second, at the time when existing plant facilities were constructed, management must have anticipated correctly the demand conditions that would stimulate optimum utilization (i.e., production at minimum average cost) and are those that actually materialized.

If these two assumptions are not valid in some situations, it is then possible that, except in industries where the coefficients of production are rigidly fixed, *capacity* (conceived of as a peak-attainment) and Hickman's *desired production rate for given investment in fixed capital* will be significantly different rates of operation. If, by some misfortune, investment in plant and equipment has become highly excessive, then the establishment may never reach

[3] Bert Hickman, "On a New Method of Capacity Estimation," *Journal of the American Statistical Association*, LIX (June 1964), 529-49.

[4] This assertion has the appearance of contradicting his earlier statement (in "Capacity, Capacity Utilization," 420) that "the question posed [for capacity research] is this: How much physical output can be produced with a given plant under a normal organization of production and with an uninterrupted and unlimited flow of variable inputs?" However, a careful examination of this quotation reveals that the maximal output referred to here would in fact be the desired output level that management had in mind when building the plant in the first place. This resolves the apparent contradiction, because such a desired output level will be at, or very close to, the minimum point on the average cost curve.

a level of production where management is dissatisfied (in the sense of wanting more) with the size of its plant.[5] In this case, any capacity estimate based on plausible future demand conditions will necessarily be less than Hickman's *desired rate of operation.*

Furthermore, if business conditions are good and improving, the managers may become dissatisfied with the amount of fixed facilities at an output that is less than capacity (as defined with reference to peak-level market conditions). That is, dissatisfaction may occur before the peak of a cyclical expansion is reached, as Hickman's work has shown. In other words, output often can continue to increase in the short run after the decision to invest in a plant expansion and can be sustained at a level higher than the investment-inducing level until the new facilities are effectively installed. If expectations are favorable, a positive decision on net investment in fixed facilities may be reached as soon as output rises, or is expected to rise, to a point where the same level of output could be produced more profitably with a larger plant and the divisibility of the equipment permits the construction of additional facilities in an amount that is appropriate either to existing or to expected conditions of demand and cost.

In short, if one wishes to conceive of capacity as an output that could be sustained rationally in the short run in a plausible market-demand situation, then his capacity estimates will under some circumstances be different from Hickman's estimates for the same list of establishments.

High utilization is not a *necessary condition* for the occurrence of a positive decision on net investment, since this investment may take place as part of a modernization program, as part of a firm's entry into new products, or as part of a firm's response in its long-range planning to its expectations about cyclical fluctuation, government policy,

---

[5] This overinvestment situation can come about either because future demand is overestimated or future variable costs are underestimated by the management.

population changes, changes in consumer tastes, and technological innovations. Furthermore, high utilization is only a *sufficient condition* for the occurrence of net investment if expectations are good (as to the continuation of high demand and tolerable labor costs), recent experience with excess capacity has not been highly unfavorable, and high utilization is sustained for a sufficient period of weeks or months to be favorably impressive to the management.

2

PROBLEMS OF
AGGREGATION AND COMPARISON

$\mathcal{I}$N ORDER to carry out a useful aggregation of an economy's capacity to produce an individual product, three conditions must be fulfilled. First, the implied demands for labor and materials must be consistent at the capacity level of production. Second, the output at the aggregated capacity level of production must be adequate in quality to meet buyer's requirements. Finally, it must be reasonable to suppose that market conditions are likely to develop under which there will exist a level of demand adequate to clear such an output from the market. This last condition becomes a crucial consideration if great duplication of facilities has developed in an industry because of product differentiation or poor investment planning.

Whenever the estimation of capacity concerns establishments with diversified outputs, it is necessary to have some knowledge of the proportions in which the various goods would be produced under conditions of full capacity-utilization. For example, will a food processor continue to produce cheese, ice cream, and powdered milk in their present proportions, or in some other proportions? Except in situations of national emergency or of rapidly developing changes in consumer preference, the simplest and best assumption is that the proportions in the line of products will remain unchanged except for normal seasonal adjustments. Furthermore, whenever some product is an intermediate good, it is likely that the ratio of this output to the others would remain fairly constant during a general expansion. When the outputs of an establishment have no technical complementarity in their use or consumption, their relative amounts are more likely to be flexible.

Sometimes it is not plausible to specify unchanging output proportions. For a firm that has a line of products which it produces on job orders with highly convertible equipment, capacity estimation can only apply to the total value of output, which is taken as the indicator of the firm's activity level.

In the event of a rapidly changing consumer-preference or technological pattern, capacity is overstated if the method of allocating joint costs in multiplant and multiple-product firms producing the affected products has become inappropriate in the sense of allocating too small a share of joint costs to the recently more important products.

Whenever an aggregative product category contains the output of some industry, A, and some other industry, B, where B's output is an input for A, the validity of an aggregative capacity estimate depends upon whether the managers in A and B have reasonably similar expectations about the price and volume of B's output in the future. (Value-added estimates are preferable to gross-value estimates here.) An aggregative estimate may involve either a single and undifferentiated product which is put out by single-product establishments, or a group of products produced only at single-product establishments, or a group of products where any or all are manufactured at multiple-product establishments. But, in any case, the individual quantities, q, or values, pq, cannot be aggregated unless these addends can be reconciled as to their implications about resource requirements and about interindustry coordination.[1]

There is no unique system for classifying products. Product groupings may be defined on the basis of similarity of raw inputs, similarity of uses for the outputs, similarity of production processes, technical complementarity of the outputs, or institutional market groupings. The general criterion in forming categories is to make them as sensitive as possible to structural changes in the economy, to the exact location in the economy of bottlenecks which could constrain or are constraining a general expansion, and to differential cyclical patterns of capacity change.

There are three requirements to be fulfilled in order to compare in an unqualified way the capacity estimates for two different dates. Strict comparability requires the definition of the estimates for the two dates with reference to (1) roughly the same structure of relative prices, (2) the same list of goods (except for changes in the output of multiple-use equipment in establishments with large lines of products), and (3) the same institutional system, that is, the patterns of business organization and motivation.

[1] The construction of such an inventory of resource requirements often necessitates adding up the money values of various specific inputs. The prices that are used in forming these money-value aggregates are assumed to be those that would be associated with economically rational production of a hypothetical capacity output. For a basic study of the problem of input aggregation, see L. R. Klein, "Macroeconomics and the Theory of Rational Behavior," *Econometrica*, XIV (April 1946), 93-108.

Because of the impossibility of constructing rigorously a proper set of purely hypothetical weights representing the pattern of private preferences or public policy goals during a future business expansion, it is necessary to use empirically derived weights in the construction of aggregative capacity indexes. The significance of capacity weights based on historical production data is affected by any actual or expected changes in the structure of private or public demand.[2] For example, production weights based on historical percentage-shares of aggregate value may fail in a study of a structural transition from peace to war. In this situation, the concern is not merely with a change over time in an index with actual-value weights, but with changes in relative capacities. Relevant changes in capacity, as the economy moves toward the pattern of production expected after the transition, will not be reflected properly in an index using historical weights. Alternative weighting schemes have definite differential effects upon the behavior of production indexes.[3]

Capacity estimation is in essence an inference about what would probably happen if a given stock of fixed plant and equipment were to exist under alternative and hypothetical market conditions that might develop in the future. This means that capacity estimates are inevitably subject to random errors because of the simplifying assumptions that are required concerning utilization at the previous peak in production, managerial goals, the rate of effective installation of new equipment, and the smoothness of the time-distribution of productivity changes. And, of course, capacity estimates are affected by such universal sources of error as incomplete data and computational mistakes and by formula bias in index number comparisons.

[2] A classic study of proper weighting for a capacity index is Henry Villard, "Some Aspects of the Concept of Capacity to Produce," *Review of Economics and Statistics,* XXI (Feb. 1939), 13-20.

[3] See, for example, U.S. Board of Governors of the Federal Reserve System, *Industrial Production,* 1959 Revision (Washington: Government Printing Office, 1960), 1-74.

19

But capacity estimates are also affected by systematic errors that tend to be generated by the various methods of estimation themselves. Systematic errors (or, more rigorously, systematic *differences* with other estimates) arise in capacity's estimation whenever a method fails to take a full account of, or deliberately excludes from consideration, one or more of the constraints upon shortrun output expansion. If the full effect of a constraint is underrated or ignored, capacity will be overstated, while if a constraint is exaggerated, capacity will be understated. More specifically, method-induced systematic errors are created whenever an estimation method either fails to allow for the effects of changes in general economic conditions upon the feasibility of higher levels of production, or uses a definition of capacity or an estimation procedure that causes disproportionate relative emphasis on the various constraints.

It is possible at this point to note that the analysis thus far has made it possible to generalize some of the difficulties that beset attempts to estimate potential GNP (where the difference between this and actual GNP is presumed to be a measure of slack or waste in the economic system) as follows:

1. Any estimate of potential GNP implies an assumed structure of relative output prices, which may or may not be the same as that associated with actual GNP.

This proposition has several corollaries, as follows:

2. The aggregate *level* of prices associated with potential GNP may not be the same as that associated with actual GNP.

3. Furthermore, sophisticated contemporary estimates of potential GNP usually involve an explicit statement of the amount of inflation that would be expected to be associated with a shortrun movement of the economic system to potential GNP.

20

4. The existence of a gap between potential and actual GNP does not necessarily imply the existence of a traditional Keynesian deflationary gap. The absence of such a rigorous correspondence can be largely explained by a multitude of ways in which the economy deviates from perfect competition *in addition to* Keynesian downward wage-rigidity.

5. Since changes in price structure imply changes in weighting, movements along the income axis in the textbook Keynesian equilibrium diagram can only be used to represent the direction of static forces and cannot be said to represent historical movement whenever such movement involves a change in price structure, because, with the implied change in value-weights, the meaning of the income axis itself changes.

6. Even if one assumes that no changes in value-weights are involved in a movement along an income axis toward a full employment point in a deflationary gap diagram, this point is ambiguous with respect to the size of the labor force, since the actual labor force and the potential labor force cannot be safely assumed to be the same thing.[4]

[4] Two representative studies on the question of potential GNP are Arthur M. Okun, "The Gap Between Actual and Potential Output," in *The Battle Against Unemployment*, ed. Arthur M. Okun (New York: W. W. Norton, 1965), 13-22, and Edwin Kuh, "Measurement of Potential Output," *American Economic Review*, LVI (Sept. 1966), 758-76.

3

EXAMPLES OF
ESTIMATION PROBLEMS

SUPPOSE that early in 1964 a certain Commerce Department official receives information that the Kennedy Round negotiations in Geneva are to bring about a great reduction of tariffs on several imports into the Common Market from the rest of the world. He notes that one of the categories to be affected is rolled photographic film for still prints. He wishes to estimate the ability of some particular American corporation to respond quickly to this future expansion of its market.

Now, suppose that he obtains the annual reports and other publications of this firm and finds to his good fortune that he has separate data for the firm's roll film division. After a careful study of this material, he establishes the following pertinent facts.

In its roll film plant the firm manufactures two sizes of film with two different photographic speeds. Since each type is produced in both a black-and-white and a color variety, the firm thus produces a total of eight individual film products. The eight varieties are produced more or less continuously, although they are all produced with the same equipment, which is perfectly convertible from one use to another. An implication of this is that the eight types of film production are competing uses for the equipment. This fact does not disturb the investigator however, because he expects that the impending widening of the market will not require any marked change from the proportions in which the eight kinds of film are presently produced.

He finds that in 1962 the average productivity of this firm's fixed capital in its roll film division was higher than at any period in the history of this establishment. He notes that during that year the depreciated book value of the plant and equipment in this division was $10,000,000 and that the company has always followed a policy of continuous replacement and maintenance by immediately plowing depreciation funds back into the plant. He also finds that during 1962 the firm made a net addition to its floor space and equipment in this division. This net investment amounted to $300,000. Although this was not effectively installed until very late in 1962, the investment decision had been made in 1961 when the climate of business expectations had been better than it was in 1962. (We are assuming no price-changes for capital goods.)

He takes pains to note that certain small but significant innovations were contained in the new equipment and that these were also present in the equipment installed since then on an ordinary replacement basis. This fact is important, because he will use the average productivity of capital goods for 1962 as the basis for his first approximation of 1965 capacity, in that he will apply the 1962 productivity ratio to the expected stock of fixed capital for 1965. The presence of the innovations will cause the first approximation to understate the capacity of the establishment.

He observes that the establishment has experienced a slump since 1962, as the following facts demonstrate. During 1962, with an average total employment of 1,200 people working in a plant worth $10,000,000, the establishment produced an output worth $7,800,000,[1] net of the value of input shipments from other divisions of the corporation and from other firms. In 1963, 1,100 employees working with a fixed-capital stock worth $10,300,000 produced only $7,500,000 worth of value-added output.

He finds a company proclamation to the effect that, at current rates, production in this division in 1964 will be only $6,000,000 and average weekly employment only 950 people. Since no net investment or disinvestment has taken place since 1962, the value of the plant is $10,300,000 (in current prices). Since no new construction, on the one hand, or reduction of replacement and maintenance, on the other, is anticipated, and since no severe inflation is expected, he may assume that the plant will have this same value in 1965.

An application of the plant's 1962 coefficient of fixed-capital productivity, 78:100, to the expected 1965 stock of fixed capital, $10,300,000 worth, yields a first approximation for 1965 capacity of $8,034,000 of value-added. Similarly, using the 1962 ratio of capital to labor, 10,000,000 dollars : 1,200 workers, on the expected 1965 stock of fixed capital gives an estimated average employment of 1,236 for 1965 if capacity is fully utilized.

Now, without laboring the hypothetical arithmetic any

[1] In a multiple-product case of this kind, economic value is preferable as a measure of output for our purposes over such measures as the number of physical units produced, weight of the output, or the spatial dimensions of shipments.

24

further, let us note some of the additional factors that our Department of Commerce official must take into account if he wishes to refine the 1965 estimate by successive approximations.

The velocity of operation physically possible for most of the equipment used in roll film manufacturing is so great that from a practical standpoint it might as well be infinite—a conclusion that is based on engineering estimates and on the fact that the more dexterous and ambitious workers produce at rates far above the average. An implication of this fact is that the main origins of inadaptability in this kind of production are: the human limitations of the average worker; the inability of the firm to provide better incentives; the departmental differences in shift conditions, which are such that although some departments work only two shifts while the departments that feed these departments work three, and three-shift departments could not, without more equipment and men, keep up if the two-shift departments added a third shift; and the extensive machinery-cleaning and output-handling requirements in the one- and two-shift departments, where these requirements are such that the maintenance workers, who work during the "down" hours, would greatly hamper the work of the operators during an extra shift. Thus, while some ordinary overtime work might be possible, the probability of large increases in employment after all equipment has been brought into regular use is very low; in spite of the high adaptability of each machine to a more intense usage, the adaptability of the establishment at large to new employment in the form of new shifts is low. For this reason, the estimated capacity is probably appropriate on the basis of adaptability considerations.

Another reason for thinking that the estimate should not be revised upward is that while the equipment used in roll film manufacturing is highly convertible (from one type of film production to another, though, of course, not from one stage to another), outright substitution of materials is impossible (with trivial exceptions). Furthermore, the tolerance of the roll film market for downward changes in the quality of output is quite low.

However, the innovations mentioned earlier (regarding the equipment installed since 1961) have the effect of making the estimated capacity an understatement. This requires a small upward revision of the estimate. Such a revision would also be required if there were any evidence of a substantial underutilization during 1962 (the productivity reference-year).

As for the reorganizational implications of the capacity estimate and the time period that would be required to reach such an annual rate of production, it seems reasonable to suppose that, if the European tariff reduction were accomplished in late 1964, say November, then the capacity rate of production could be achieved within four or five months.

The estimate is, of course, slightly too low to the extent that output prices for roll film may be expected to rise during the period to which the estimate applies. That is, if demand is increasing in the domestic market in such a way that the firm could successfully command a higher price on each product, and if it could maintain this price in the face of foreign competition in the new free-trade situation, then the shortrun profit-maximizing output is shifted to a higher level. The possible increase will be slight, however, because of the previously mentioned low adaptability of the equipment to additional amounts of labor after regular-use is achieved.

The estimate is too high to the extent that the firm will face higher input prices, especially wages. It is also too high to the degree that either credit conditions or the firm's financial position is unfavorable (although neither of these is likely to affect the typical large corporation negatively under business conditions which are generally favorable).

Suppose that our hypothetical public official wishes to

aggregate his estimate for this company, say Company A, with similar estimates for the other companies in this industry, say Company B and Company C. He is careful not to proceed by simply totaling the value-added of the three companies, because, in the first place, he notes that each produces goods other than rolled films, and, in the second place, he finds that the lines of products are not identical anyway. A is unique among the three in that it produces industrial chemicals not only for its own use but also for the market. B has a line of optical equipment with which A and C, though they manufacture cameras, do not compete. C has a national monopoly in flat film and indoor lighting equipment. With all this in mind, the official makes estimates only for the roll film establishment or division within each firm, and by this he confines himself to a sufficiently specific and consistent line of products. He takes care to see that the individual estimates for each establishment can be reconciled with one another as to their implied input requirements and as to the effective coordination of intraindustry shipments of intermediate products (since he knows that B and C buy large quantities of chemicals from A).

Since the tautology that capacity is the output which an establishment *can produce* may be interpreted in a variety of ways, there are a number of distinct concepts of capacity which are in use by economists, businessmen, and others. The model developed in the two previous chapters affirms the logical possibility of a multiplicity of capacity concepts, since it shows that a definite concept of capacity requires a specification of values for an entire list of variables. The diversity of concepts sometimes has been a source of unnecessary controversy, especially about alleged differences between efficiency and maximization, and so it is worthwhile to examine briefly some of the concepts of economic capacity.

For example, de Leeuw has recognized three significant

27

concepts of economic capacity.[2] They are based on different terms. One has the schedule of production as its frame of reference, another is defined in terms of behavior of average costs, and the third is based on the behavior of marginal costs.

The first concept is developed from an idea of normal practice. Normal practice is thought of as the manpower and scheduling arrangement which has been typical of recent peaceful and prosperous years. Output under this schedule is thought of as capacity. As de Leeuw points out, the significance of such a capacity output is hard to assess, for full utilization of normal-practice capacity might sometimes involve pressure for new investment, while under other conditions it might be carried on without generating decisions for net capital formation. A distinguishing feature of this type of concept is that level-of-utilization is defined on the basis of the time-in-use of inputs rather than on the basis of the physical quantities of the inputs or the cost of drawing flows of services from them. Some number of hours of utilization is simply designated as full utilization; capacity is then the output associated with this work schedule under normal conditions of productivity.

A second way to construe the term capacity, according to de Leeuw, is in terms of efficient operation—more precisely, as the minimum point on a shortrun average total cost curve. The same difficulty occurs with this concept as with the normal-practice approach, as de Leeuw recognizes. Some industries may experience pressure for net investment immediately when operation is at capacity, while others may not until output is well beyond capacity.

The third concept recognized by de Leeuw appears to be an original one.[3] He proposes to define capacity as

[2] Frank de Leeuw, "The Concept of Capacity," in American Statistical Association, 1961 Proceedings of the Business and Economic Statistics Section (Washington: American Statistical Association, 1961), 324-25.
[3] Ibid.

28

that output for which shortrun marginal costs are x percent above current minimum shortrun average total costs, where x would be determined by the excess that empirical evidence would indicate to be necessary to exert an impact on the capital goods industries. With this definition, a rate of utilization at or near 100 percent would necessarily be a precursor of net investment. This concept has the advantage, as he notes, of making it clear that a workable concept of capacity must embody not one but several shortrun limitations upon the level of production. These are the constraints created by fixed plant, the labor force (employed and available), and the availability of materials and credit. (These constraints, of course, are only significant with reference to definite managerial goals and expectations.)

Zabel sees a different kind of plurality of capacity concepts.[4] For him the diversity is created by the attempt to specify an estimation procedure. He recognizes three types of estimates, where the classification is based on the level of aggregation involved in the estimate and the use to be made of it. These categories are (1) estimates for a single establishment or for a group of establishments making up an industry; (2) estimates for all establishments in a national economy, with due account taken of the interdependencies associated with simultaneous high level production by all these units; and (3) estimates made for an economy or sector thereof by using the relationship between output and new investment which is contained in some econometric model of investment behavior. Now, while these three approaches are not necessarily inconsistent, a careful enumeration of the constraints that an estimator has in mind when he chooses an approach would show that all three approaches can involve different concepts of what capacity is. Zabel notes that at first glance they respectively

[4] Edward Zabel, "Concepts and Measurements of Productive Capacity" (unpublished Ph.D. dissertation, Princeton University, 1956), 17 ff.

29

suggest the ideas of (1) maximization of output, (2) efficient production in a general equilibrium of the national economy, and (3) an investment-trigger rate of production.

One reason for the multiplicity of concepts is that the idea of capacity has been used in the economic literature in substantially different kinds of arguments. Diverse sets of connotations, each of which may be appropriate in a particular argument, tend to lurk as an unnoticed source of confusion. It is sometimes uncertain whether a writer or speaker is thinking of the maximum physical capability of a fixed input, or of any possible output for a given stock of plant and equipment, or of the optimum output for an establishment, or of the output obtainable under some kind of emergency scheduling, or of something else. That different kinds of research involve different usages of the term *capacity* becomes especially clear if one ponders the distinctions between excess capacity resulting from imperfections in competition, unused capacity that is necessary for flexibility because of seasonal or erratic fluctuations, unused capacity resulting from a serious recession, and idle capacity resulting from obsolescence.

In this connection, it is interesting to speculate on what a manufacturer means by capacity when he says that he is operating at less than capacity. He does not ordinarily mean the maximum physical product of his fixed capital, although in some cases this may not be far from what he has in mind. Nor is he likely to be thinking of output at economic equilibrium under current conditions, for he is inclined to speculate about the possibilities for his plant under hypothetical conditions of market demand. In view of the fact that he probably holds fairly definite expectations about future input costs, the point which he probably thinks of as full capacity is that output beyond which average total costs would increase sharply. It is of course partly determined by his expectations about the way factor prices would behave under an increased demand for them.

It is important to note that, in spite of the conflicting

connotations carried by the term *capacity*, a common theme is often present in the term's usage. It is the idea that capacity is a rate of production which could be attained rationally under certain hypothetical conditions. It is an output level that is constrained by existing goals and recognizable bottlenecks.

It is also important to note that in capacity research there is no basis for a categorical distinction between maximization and optimization. Human behavior is always subject to constraints (Pareto's *les obstacles*) and driven by motives that are expressable as a pattern of preferences (Pareto's *les gouts*[5]). That which maximizes goal attainment also economizes.

Students of capacity sometimes make a distinction between a *maximal* concept of capacity and an *optimal* concept. But what really lies under this distinction is not any inherent difference between maximization and optimization, but rather a difference in the conditions (of market demand and cost of variable inputs) which are assumed to be associated with capacity-level production.

A *questionnaire* survey on capacity may be said to be open-ended if the questionnaire does not provide a definition of capacity for the respondent to use; that is, if it allows each respondent to use a concept which to him seems appropriate. The McGraw-Hill sample survey is an example of this.[6] This project has grown out of an attempt to explain investment behavior, and its data are simply numbers indicating what plant managers think capacity is. It appears that the respondents in this survey usually think of capacity as the maximum output obtainable with normal work schedules, and that they have a preferred rate of operation which

[5] Vilfredo Pareto, *Manuel d'économie politique* (Paris: Marcel Giard, 1927), *passim.*
[6] Margaret Matulis, "Capacity and Operating Rates," in American Statistical Association, *1961 Proceedings of the Business and Economic Statistics Section* (Washington: American Statistical Association, 1961), 306-308.

is a little less than this. Since the McGraw-Hill investigators are more concerned with relative changes in capacity over time than with the actual magnitude of capacity, it is more important for each firm in the sample to be consistent in its definition as time passes than for all firms to use the same definition. In any case, since McGraw-Hill cannot compel a company to respond, the investigators believe that the number of responses would decrease if the questionnaire specified a concept of capacity. They work under the conviction that a large response to a vague question is more useful than a small response to a precise question, especially since the sample is not drawn randomly from a preestablished frame (i.e., list of the entire population of firms). This is important, since the frequency-distributions of establishment-capacities for the various industries are not known.

The fact that the McGraw-Hill survey is not based on a random sample needs to be stressed. It is not possible to compute a sampling error from the means of the random samples of a given size which could be drawn from the population, since these samples have not been drawn. And since the standard deviation for the entire population is not known, it is furthermore not possible to attach any particular significance to the shape or dispersion of the frequency distribution of the sample that is used. On top of this the data used by McGraw-Hill in constructing aggregative utilization percentages have been drawn from two different sources, the McGraw-Hill questionnaire and a Federal Reserve survey of production, which are based on nonequivalent lists of firms.

The McGraw-Hill questionnaire requests that the companies in the sample report only net increases in capacity and that these increases represent acquisition of "brand new" facilities (so that purchases of used equipment will not affect the estimates). However, there are other sources of error with which it is not so easy to cope, as the McGraw-Hill researchers recognize. For example, one cannot be sure that a respondent will include the effects of productivity-increasing improvements that exist in machinery bought simply to replace old equipment. Also, replacement equipment is to some degree really a net addition anyway if the firm continues to use occasionally its "replaced" equipment (which can happen if the old equipment is merely obsolete and not worn out). Furthermore, a movement into a new line of goods might be reported as an increase in capacity with no concurrent increase in the firm's fixed capital or employment.

In general, there are reasons for a good deal of pessimism about the probable success of questionnaire surveys on capacity, even when they are not open-ended. While it is true that the Annual Survey of Manufactures (or some other sample survey based on as comprehensive a frame) could be adapted so that all respondents would be confronted with questions on capacity, the estimates received would often not have any reasonable degree of accuracy or significance. It is true that the questionnaire used in the Annual Survey gets information on the kind of statistical items that would have to be mentioned in a capacity questionnaire, especially if it is not open-ended. But it deals with these variables (such as inventory behavior, outlay for plant and equipment, energy consumed, materials consumed, book value of assets, employment, manhours, and value of shipments) as historical facts and not as conjectured magnitudes which are part of a hypothetical business situation. I seriously question whether the respondents in this and other manufacturing surveys have at hand the information that is necessary for them to make useful estimates of their future behavior, especially in terms of aggregatable estimates. In 1920 and 1923 the Census of Manufactures included questions on capacity but failed to get good responses or, in some cases, any response at all, and the effort was subsequently abandoned.

There are other reasons for pessimism about the ability of respondents to give the kind of information required. In the first place, the concept of capacity can only be made successfully operational in a questionnaire survey if each respondent is conscious of the thought process by which he makes his decisions on the level and content of production (since only then can he carefully estimate his behavior in a hypothetical situation) and if this thought process remains fairly stable as time passes. Furthermore, a researcher may have a concept of capacity which is not operational (as far as questionnaire surveys are concerned) because of being too complicated for the respondent to use. That is, the respondent may not be trained to carry out the calculations required. He may be unwilling, or even conceivably unable, to incur the cost of the computations. And he may be uncertain about what the productivity of his inputs would be under the more intense usage coming with expanded operation and about whether the behavior of his input markets during the hypothetical expansion would actually conform to the assumptions he is told to make or must make himself in order that he may arrive at his estimate.

The National Industrial Conference Board estimates of capacity are computed from output and capital-stock data which are tabulated jointly as capital-output ratios.[7] Capacity is defined as the output that will trigger investment outlays which are directly for the purpose of making net additions to the level of output. One-hundred percent utilization is regarded as being the equivalent of the McGraw-Hill *preferred operating rate*.

The NICB procedure has been to construct a capital-output ratio (for fixed capital only) for each of twenty-eight industry groups for some year of virtually full utilization of capacity. This year is referred to as a base-year or benchmark. The ratio so constructed is then applied to the stock of fixed capital in later periods to estimate capacity in those periods; that is, if fixed capital for a particular period is

[7] Daniel Creamer, *Recent Changes in Manufacturing Capacity* (New York: National Industrial Conference Board, 1962).

placed in the numerator of the fraction, then capacity is the unknown in the denominator which will preserve the value of the capital-output ratio constructed for the base-year.

There are a couple of points of logic concerning the use of capital-output ratios in estimating capacity which need to be made clear at this point. No matter how carefully one compiles independent evidence to show that a certain benchmark year was a period of virtually full utilization, ultimately he is assuming rather than demonstrating that this was so. Thus, capital-output-ratio methods really beg the question of estimation. One can use a capital-output ratio to estimate capacity in a given period only if he accepts the rate of production during the base-year as a definition of the capacity of the stock of fixed capital during the base period, or more precisely the capacity of the establishments having that capital stock. Furthermore, since a capacity estimate is associated with an assumed milieu of business conditions, it must further be assumed that business conditions can hardly be expected ever to be much better than they were during the base period.

This last point means that the application of a capital-output ratio for a benchmark year to the capital stock for another year, with due account taken of net investment and of changes in the value of the capital stock, cannot, strictly speaking, be said to measure potential output. While this gives a rough indication of the constraining effects of the stock of fixed capital, it must be remembered that a capital-output ratio as measured at a previous peak in business activity is merely a historical fact. An output computed from that ratio and a more recent stock of capital can be said to represent potential output only if the same configuration of relative costs and prices is expected to exist during the next expansion, and if due account has been taken of the effects of changes in technology, capital-goods prices, and the capital-labor ratio upon the significance of the capital-output ratio.

It would, of course, be exceedingly difficult, if not impossible, to specify a complete set of consistent hypothetical prices (with which one could rigorously assign a value to a capacity output) which would define the profit situation that would induce full utilization. This is true even if one simply takes prices at the previous peak to be the hypothetical set. But a capacity estimate only has its meaning with reference to some fairly definite structure of input and output prices. The conclusion which arises then is that in interpreting a capacity estimate, it is important to remember that it does not represent an output which would be feasible under all possible contingencies of cost and revenue.

One experimental capacity index (prepared by the staff of the Federal Reserve Board) which was apparently based on an engineering concept tended to involve higher values for capacity, lower utilization percentages, and greater proportional changes in capacity than other estimates.[8] The sample of comparisons was too small to permit generalization, but if this was in fact a general tendency it may have been the result of a possible characteristic deemphasis of the roles of profitability constraints (and managerial goals in general) in the engineering concept of capacity.

If machine ratings are to be used in preparing a capacity estimate, some criterion must be established for dealing with idle machinery. Generally speaking, this means that some speculation must be made in each case as to whether a particular piece of equipment could be operated economically under the hypothetical conditions that are assumed in making the capacity estimate. Furthermore, if the estimate is to involve aggregation of products produced on multipurpose equipment, then either the nature of the allocation of machine-time must be taken into account or there must be an awareness of the fact that "aggregate-value" capacity

[8] De Leeuw, "The Concept of Capacity," 321, and Creamer, *Recent Changes*, 41.

and total "individual-product" capacity may not accord with each other.

Care must always be taken to account for any peculiarities in particular industries as to scheduling, scheduling possibilities, and seasonality.

Nourse and his associates in a Brookings project[9] added work scheduling as a variable in computing their *practical capacity* (vs. *rated capacity*) for those industries where feasible alternatives existed with respect to scheduling. For example, capacity for anthracite coal production was computed on the basis of a 304- as well as a 274-day work-year.

If an industry traditionally operates for only part of the year (as is the case in some lines of food canning) or at least experiences, as a matter of routine, great seasonal fluctuations in employment and production (as is the case in retailing, tourism, and some other service industries), then it is necessary to estimate the industry's capacity with this in mind. It would not make sense to estimate the number of crates of spinach that a cannery could put out working on a full-time, twelve-month schedule, for such a number would have no relation to what might actually be produced under conceivable circumstances.

In general, the capacity of an industry depends upon the time-distribution of demand in that industry. An industry may be able to increase its economic capacity simply by inducing its customers to distribute their demands more evenly; or conversely, the economic capacity of an industry may be reduced if customers suddenly insist on concentrating their demand in certain time intervals.

Since production ordinarily involves a multiplicity of different facilities, the significance of unused equipment is not always clear. Unused equipment is not necessarily excessive equipment, since in order for the production of a good or service

[9] Edwin G. Nourse and others, *America's Capacity to Produce* (Washington: Brookings Institution, 1934), esp. 18-28.

to proceed efficiently and without disruption it may be necessary for a particular component to be idle from time to time. For example, in railroading, capacity is affected by miles of track, number of terminals, tractive capacity of locomotives, and rated capacity of the rolling stock, and it is doubtful that the balance of these facilities would ever be such as to leave them all in use all of the time. It is especially important in examining a multiproduct establishment not to label unused facilities automatically as excess capacity. In such establishments it is unlikely that the pattern of demand, time-distribution of orders, and convertibility of facilities would ever be such that all equipment would be in use simultaneously. The balance of facilities is simply not that perfect. Furthermore, in an industry whose output is essentially a service (as in, say, the provision of offstreet parking), the ability to give a high quality of service may actually depend upon the existence of a permanent pool of idle equipment or space, even though individual facilities may rotate in and out of this pool.

While we say that an establishment has such-and-such capacity at a given instant, it must be remembered that capacity is not an immediately achievable output and that the time period which one would mean to allow for adjustments is in fact one of the constraints. Moving up to a capacity output, in the event that the business situation changes so as to make this a rational output, would require time and possibly some outright reorganization. It seems that during the depths of a recession the necessary adjustment period and the reorganizational requirements for reaching even an optimal (i.e., minimum average total cost) output might be rather substantial. There would be administrative delays; redirection of some input-flows might be necessary; and price changes might have to occur in the market in order to induce a movement toward capacity in any case.

The time needed and the reorganization required to

reach capacity varies throughout the business cycle, since the discrepancy between capacity and actual output varies. Capacity, as estimated by currently practiced methods of peak-forward extrapolation, while it may represent an investment-trigger level of output, does not for any highly technical industry in the depths of a recession represent a quickly achievable alternative output level. The assumed adjustment period in such a case must be taken to be rather lengthy, say forty-five to ninety days.

Two important questions regarding the validity of a trend line for capacity which is drawn from a previous peak in production (and sloped according to some known or assumed time-rate and time-pattern of net fixed-capital investment, effectively installed) are whether or not the peak output represents full utilization and whether, in any case, it involves the same degree of capacity utilization as do other peak outputs. To the extent that utilization is not full at the peak, capacity so estimated is understated. To the extent that peaks vary as to the degree of utilization, the capacity estimates are unreliable. Note, however, that these propositions assume that there is some *additional* measure of capacity.

4

THE LOGIC
OF CAPACITY ESTIMATION

$\mathcal{I}_T$ IS important to have reasonable assurance that an argument about economic capacity is logically complete; that is, that it takes into account all the variables that are in the conceptual model which is implied by the definition of capacity. The following discussion is devoted to an examination of this question.

A capacity output for a manufacturing firm is determined by placing successive restrictions upon the set of all positive, rational, integral, and finite numbers, where any number in the set is taken to be an unambiguously defined physical or value outflow of a productive activity.

The process of successive restriction is continued until a unique number, or some sufficiently narrow range of numbers, is defined. Each restriction in effect delineates a subset of the original set. Each of the subsets is dependent upon a larger set. A dependent set is one that is completely contained in a larger set and is defined in some manner as a category or group of special cases in this larger set. Some of the pairs of subsets of the original set are independent in that neither member of the pair is defined explicitly or by implication as a subset of the other. Independent sets overlap if they are defined so as to make the argument more, not less, nearly determinate. Thus the process of successive restriction and exclusion proceeds by forming subcategories and only partially compatible restrictions until a sufficiently narrow subset is formed, where this subset's member(s) has the unique property that it satisfies the requirements of alternative chains of exclusion. Capacity is indeed merely a point satisfying successive restrictions.

This means that we take an inventory of the various properties with which we wish to endow the capacity output and then form successively smaller restraining subsets as well as subsets that are only partially consistent with each other, until an output is determined. Let A represent all positive, rational, integral, and finite outputs and B_1, B_2, B_3, and B_4 represent subsets defined by chains of successive restrictions. B_2 is a subset of B_1, and B_4 is a subset of B_3. The intersection of B_2 and B_4 is a subset, C, of A and contains only a single number.

This is to say that

$$C = B_4 \cap B_2, \tag{1}$$

where

$$B_4 \subset B_3, \tag{2}$$

$$B_2 \subset B_1, \tag{3}$$

$$B_3 \subset A, \tag{4}$$

and

$$B_1 \subset A. \tag{5}$$

Let γ represent the single member of C, where this member is capacity by definition. Then

41

$$C = \{\gamma\} = \cap B_1, B_2, B_3, B_4 = B_1 \cap B_2 \cap B_3 \cap B_4 \quad (6)$$

or more generally,

$$\gamma = \cap B_i, \quad i = 1, 2, \ldots, n. \quad (7)$$

This illustrates the process of argumentation on capacity. A, B_1, B_2 is a chain of exclusion, where B_2 is dependent upon B_1 and is a subclass thereof. The formation of B_2 makes the argument more nearly determinate, because it narrows the range of outputs under consideration. B_1 and B_3 are independent, in that they are parts of different chains of exclusion. Taken together, they make the argument more nearly determinant, since they are only partially consistent. The formation of any subset that is identical with some other set adds nothing to the argument, because it does not go any further than any previous restriction. If any subset, D, is totally inconsistent with the other subsets, it represents an internal contradiction in the definition of capacity. It is possible for different measures of capacity, of course, to employ inconsistent sets in the definition of capacity. But this fact alone is sufficient to make two series of estimates behave differently.

The exact sizes of the subsets are ambiguous when taken separately. They become definite when considered together as a pattern of constraints. For example, we assert that possible output is constrained by the shortrun production function. That is, we exclude from the set of all outputs those outputs that are not consistent with this particular function. But this does not mean that we can take this constraint alone and actually enumerate the membership of the subset that conforms to it. The size of this subset is quite ambiguous until we know the other constraints, such as the amount of fixed equipment. But, each constraint that appears in the model necessarily excludes certain levels of production from consideration in managerial planning for output expansion.

In short, a capacity argument consists of defining subsets $B_1, \ldots, B_n$ in economic terms. The model contains two chains of exclusion, which may be thought of as the subsets $B_1, \ldots, B_i$ and $B_j, \ldots, B_n$. Consider the economic meaning of the two chains of exclusion.

One chain expresses all those constraints that arise because we fix a time period, x days, to which any firm in the economy is to be limited in its adjustment of output and a date of reference on which the supposed adjustment would begin. That is, the first subset contains all those levels of output that a given firm could conceivably reach by means of an x day adjustment beginning on some given day. The purposes for defining this subset are to indicate that the capacity number which is to be determined by the argument will have the property that it can be attained by the firm within x days and to fix certain conditions and relations both within the firm and in the economy at large. By fixing a time period for adjustment we are necessarily saying that certain stocks of production resources in the firm (i.e., legally internal) and in the economy at large (i.e., legally external), on the basis of past experience, will have to be regarded as being fixed in supply during that time period. All of the subsets of this first subset, some of which overlap and are of different sizes, consist of plausible ranges of potential output levels.

The second chain of exclusion is the specification of those psychological and political conditions in the economy which must be assumed to be in existence during and following the adjustment period. These are to be thought of as conditions that do not in themselves result from the fixing of a time period. They pertain to private market demand for final outputs, managerial aspirations, public demand for final outputs, and public policies relating to monetary regulation, price controls, subsidization, and wage controls.

Thus there are two definitive restrictions in the determination of capacity. They are definitive in that they fix the only constraints that must be postulated. All other constraints follow from them, either by implication or by subclassification. Once the two definitive constraints are made definite, capacity is determined by implication. That is, as we proceed by successive restriction to exclude outputs from the original set and to seek out the physical or behavioral expressions of these restrictions, we find that there are two general constraints, "time" and "policy conditions," which either imply the specific constraints or contain them as subcategories.

By "time" as a constraint we mean that one of the things that must be specified in a definition of capacity is the time period that is to be allowed to the firm for reorganization. A meaningful capacity indicates an output that is an obtainable flow after a certain given reorganization period and in a certain policy climate, either actual or hypothetical. This is one of the two grand restrictions. The specific constraints implied by it are not in themselves sufficient to determine capacity, but they are necessary. (In order for capacity to be determinate, the other grand restriction, "policy conditions in the economy," and its corollaries, must be added.) A capacity estimate depends upon certain things being fixed and upon the rules governing the relationship of variable magnitudes to these fixed entities. Fixing the time period, which will be called the short run, necessarily implies that there are certain things which will have to be regarded as fixed stocks because they cannot be varied during that time period; their reorganizational requirements are too complex for such rapid variation. Each of these stocks is a constraint. Thus it is in the determination of fixed stocks of inputs that the specification of a time period is crucial in the definition of capacity.

For the economy as a whole the quantities of certain resources are fixed in the short run. But how can such a limitation in the economy constrain the capacity of a firm, if the firm regards the resource in question as a variable input? The demands upon this resource by various firms must be consistent. While the firm will indeed regard this resource as a variable input, it will nonetheless compete

44

with other firms for this resource, and with increasing intensity as output expands. Competition for the pool of this scarce resource implies that this input will have a price, and thus a cost, to the firm. Even if the pool of a resource can be augmented during the period of adjustment, this good will still have a cost when used by the firm. The firm merely experiences this particular stock constraint by way of an intermediate variable, the price of the input. The imposition of a time constraint fixes the quantities of certain resources in the economy at large; that is, it fixes a pattern of scarcities. An increasing need for such resources would likely lead to increases in their prices. Expected increases in factor prices are important factors in the determination of the capacity of a firm.

The fixing of a time constraint will also freeze the technology in the economy and probably also the specific processes used by firms. In some cases it will limit changes in the schedule of production.

It is true that the "external" stocks affect "policy conditions in the economy." But we distinguish "external" stock constraints from "policy conditions," because we wish to separate the former from those economic conditions that arise solely from demand, expectations, business aspirations, and public policy goals, none of which arise directly from the specification of a time period.

It is not always possible to maintain a perfect separation of the two categories, nor even always to keep specific constraints within each category separated. This is because of several complications in the process of successive restriction. First, there is a cross-relationship between some pairs of subsets where each member of the pair lies in a different chain of exclusion. That is to say, there are cases where the nature of a restriction defined on one side of the argument affects the nature of a restriction defined on the other side of the argument. Thus, it is necessary to discuss such subsets together, in order to develop a realistic picture of managerial decision-making. (There are two instances of this. The first has to do with input prices as constraints in production planning. Conditions affecting these prices can arise in either chain of exclusion. The stock of human and other resources affects input prices, but these prices are also influenced by public policy and law. These distinct kinds of constraints act together in the firm's decision-making and are more than likely indistinguishable to the firm. Thus they are considered together. This problem also arises in connection with those constraints created by the financial position of the firm. It is apparent that constraints which are analytically very different in that they come from different sources act together and are indistinguishable in a firm's decision-making.) Generally stated, the problem is that sometimes very diverse influences are merged into a single variable in a firm's decision-making. There is a second complication. Sometimes even subsets within the same chain of exclusion have to be considered simultaneously, because a firm's decisions on one variable cannot be made independently of its decisions on some other variable. Thus, as a case in point, it is not possible in the final analysis to deal with the employment of capital goods and labor separately.

Let us outline the two chains of exclusion. The first is as follows. By fixing a time period for adjustment and a date of application for the period to begin, we also fix

(1) n stocks of productive goods within the firm, which the firm cannot vary during the given period because of technical complexities or contractual obligation, and n depreciation rates, salaries, rental rates, and so on, for these stocks,

(2) m prices which the firm must pay for productive inputs that it can employ on a variable basis during the period of adjustment,

(3) a reservoir of internal financial resources, which the firm will already have at its disposal during the adjustment period, and

(4) certain shortrun limitations upon changes in method of production in particular and factor adaptation in general.

Restriction (4) is not necessarily distinct from (1). Each of these restrictions in some way limits the range from which a firm may select a target output in planning for shortrun expansion. The second group of propositions consists of a set of hypotheses about human behavior. Each hypothesis concerns an assumption that should be made in computing a capacity output. A determinate argument about capacity must include assumptions concerning

(5) any increase in output price (or any other signal of increased demand),

(6) any possibilities for cost-plus contracting or subsidization,

(7) the minimum quality of output that would be tolerated by the users of the product,

(8) the money supply, the interest rate, the credit conditions generally,

(9) cost controls by public authority, and

(10) the de facto managerial aspirations within the firm as to profit, total revenue, output, financial integrity, and so on.

It remains to be shown that this set of restrictions is sufficient in number to determine a competent managerial decision on shortrun output expansion. How may we know that the list of constraints and interactions is complete? The test for completeness is found by turning to the formal definition of capacity. We formally define the capacity of a manufacturing firm as (*a*) *an output* that could be produced (*b*) *in the short run under hypothetical conditions* by (*c*) *a designated collection of inputs* each of which would have (*d*) *a cost.* The two chains of exclusion specify (*a*) the content of the output and its quality, (*b*) the goals that

TABLE 1

Capacity Indexes for Manufacturing

Index	Operational Definition	Economic Concept	Significance of O_c Series
Census[a]	$O_c = O_{ppAS} \cdot (1 + r_K)$	cyclical peak	reasonable
NICB	$O_c = (O/K)_{pp} \cdot K$	cyclical peak	reasonable
Wharton	$O_c = O_{ppFR} \cdot (1 + r_{oFR}) \cdot k_{KP}$	cyclical peak	reasonable
McGraw-Hill	$O_c = O_{MH}/U_{MH} = O_{dMH}/U_{dMH}$	not clear	uncertain
FRB	$O_c = O_{FR}/U_{MH}$	not clear	impressive
Brookings[b]	$O_c = O_d = f(K_d) \equiv f(K + I)$	desired normal output	reasonable
OBE[c]	$O_c \gtreqqless O_d$	desired normal output	reasonable

48

Variables

O = output
K = stock of capital
U = utilization percentage
r = rate of growth
k = correction for systematic bias
I = net investment

Subscripts

c = capacity
o = output
κ = stock of capital
pp = previous peak
d = designation that variable in question is estimate of subjective aspiration held by manufacturers rather than actually observed quantity
κP = Klein-Preston adjustment for bias, where this adjustment is based upon aggregate production function; see *American Economic Review*, LVII (March 1967), 34-58

AS = Annual Survey data
FR = Federal Reserve data
MH = McGraw-Hill data

---

[a] See U.S. Bureau of the Census, *The Measurement of Performance Potential in Manufacturing Establishments* (Washington: Government Printing Office, 1965).

[b] K_d is estimated by studying responses of net investment to output changes. See Bert Hickman, "On a New Method of Capacity Estimation," *Journal of the American Statistical Association*, LIX (June 1964), 529-49.

[c] The OBE project consists of ordinal, not cardinal, measurement; the Office of Business Economics simply tries to ascertain whether managers feel that present capacity is equal to, greater than, or less than desired normal output. See *Survey of Current Business*, XLVII (June 1967), 7-10.

would dictate shortrun managerial decisions on the level of operation and the external parameters that pertain to such decisions, (c) the fixed and variable inputs that are employed in the execution of such decisions, and (d) the cost of using such inputs. Thus the two series of restrictions are adequate.

If the literature on United States productive capacity is studied in terms of the analysis in this chapter, a set of conclusions may be stated for each of the major contemporary capacity indexes for American manufacturing. These conclusions consist of an explicit statement of the operational definition of capacity which is employed; a statement of the economic concept of capacity which is involved in the operational definition; and a subjective judgment about the usefulness (i.e., empirically demonstrated significance) of the index in question, as to its explanatory and predictive power in the study of business behavior, and its conformity in its pattern of trend and fluctuation with other indexes of capacity and with indexes of capital-stock behavior, and are set forth in Table 1.

The difference between the behavior of any two alternative capacity indexes must, for the economist to concern himself with it, be large enough to be of some consequence for decisions that are made in the application of public policy. Indeed, it seems that this relevance or lack of relevance of some difference provides the most useful criterion for deciding whether to refer to said difference as "large" or "small"; if there is no administrative or social-philosophical significance of a difference in index behavior, the difference is "small." Continuing this line of reasoning, we say that a difference is "characteristic" if it not only is "large" but also is merely one member of a time series of such differences. However, for purposes of clarity it needs to be pointed out that two indexes may exhibit a characteristic difference as far as the magnitude of capacity or its utilization is concerned and yet still show the same pattern of growth or fluctuation as far as direction of movement is concerned. And so, the definition of "small" differences needs to be made more rigorous; we say that a difference is "small" if two indexes support the same conclusion not only about the direction of a policy action (assuming a policy philosophy to be in existence, of course) but also about its magnitude. In short, the fact that two indexes tend to move in the same direction does not by necessity mean that there are no "large" (that is, scientifically interesting) differences between them.

The pertinent implication of these remarks is that there may be some numerical differences in the behavior of capacity indexes that should not, and in fact cannot, be taken seriously. Seen from this perspective, and in view of the difficulties in constructing and computing capacity indexes, there is a pleasing degree of agreement in the behavior of some of the existing published estimates, and the reference in the preface of this book to "the frequent failure of estimates prepared by different methods to be in agreement" loses some, although certainly not all, of its significance. One's willingness to be comfortable with "small" differences is strengthened by the fact that the present state of the literature on capacity is such that it is sometimes exceedingly difficult for a reader to know how to interpret the observed differences, in that the publications often do not give a complete list of assumptions that specify the determinants of capacity. The central purpose of this monograph is to show that a meaningful and confident interpretation of the economic significance of a capacity estimate or index depends upon one's being conscious of these assumptions. Serious students of economic problems often waste their energy trying to interpret differences between published estimates of capacity solely on the basis of incomplete published information about the preparation of these estimates. Perhaps a short exercise in index interpretation will be helpful. Consider the data in Table 2.

TABLE 2

Alternative Capacity Indexes[a]

1955-1957; 1953 = 100

Year	Hickman (Variant I[b])	Federal Reserve Board	NICB	Fortune	McGraw-Hill
1955	110	108	110	107	114
1956	115	114	115	113	121
1957	121	119	118	119	128

[a] Compiled from Hickman, "On a New Method of Capacity Estimation," 547, and Almarin Phillips, "An Appraisal of Measures of Capacity," *American Economic Review*, LIII (May 1963), 281.

[b] Based on direct use of aggregated investment data rather than aggregation of separately prepared industry indexes.

The differences between the drifts in the Hickman, Federal Reserve, NICB, and Fortune indexes do not seem to be of much consequence so far as public policy is concerned. (The validity of this assertion, however, depends upon the assumption that the base-year capacity estimates upon which the indexes rest are not different in the "large" sense. My search of the literature has not yielded any information on this point.) This is not to say that the differences between these four series result solely from random errors. (More than likely, the differences, though "small," are systematic, in that they are probably the result of differences in coverage and of conscious or unconscious conceptual differences.) It is simply to say that it is impossible to tell from the published literature alone whether and why this is or is not the case.

Concerning comparisons between the behavior of any of these four indexes and the fifth—the McGraw-Hill index— the differences seem clearly to be significant, that is, "large." The behavior shown for the McGraw-Hill index has different implications about how well the American economy was doing in forming capacity (and, conversely, about how "badly" it was doing in creating what was shortly to become excess capacity during the 1957-1958 recession). But, here again it is impossible for the "outsider" to know what causal significance to attach to this difference in behavior, since the full set of implicit assumptions pertaining to the determinants of capacity is not given in the relevant publications.

In closing, consider two points. First, because of differences in survey coverage, averaging, rounding, and basing, one cannot reasonably expect the magnitudes of capacity and its utilization as computed by the various methods to coincide in every instance, but it is reasonable to hope for the relative movements of the indexes to be the same. For example, while the McGraw-Hill and NICB indexes[1] support the same conclusions about the extent of excess capacity in manufacturing at the 1957 and 1959 peaks and in the last quarter of 1961, the agreement for particular industries is not close. For 1959, only ten of the thirteen industries for which comparison is possible were shown to be in the same state of affairs as to the presence or absence of excess capacity. For 1961, only eight industries received the same classification on the existence of excess capacity. With regard to relative movements of utilization percentages for industry groups, the correspondence between the McGraw-Hill and NICB series is even less. In half of fifty year-to-year comparisons of the utilization percentages, the two measures move in different directions. Only rarely during this period is there an agreement on the amplitude of fluctuations.

Second, the normal tendency of the increasingly sophisticated Federal Reserve utilization percentage to run at less than 90 percent (see *Federal Reserve Bulletin*, Nov. 1966, pp. 1605-15), even during periods of prosperity, clearly and pointedly illustrates the point that the meaning of 100 percent utilization is relative to the measure in question.

Indeed, it would not be useful to prove deductively

[1] See Creamer, *Recent Changes*, 36-42, for the data discussed in this paragraph.

that the concept of capacity defines a measurable attribute, because after formulating a proof one would find that he was no better off than before. *Capacity* is a symbol for *a hypothetical output*, and all that such a proof would show is that certain a priori definitions and empirical generalizations do indeed imply a relationship between certain hypothetical conditions and the level of production. More fundamentally, the general economic and political significance of a capacity index depends upon considerations outside the logic of the index itself, that is, upon the significance of the index's assumptions within the framework of some given economic, political, or sociological theory of human behavior.

INDEX

Aggregation: prerequisites for, 16, 17, 18
Annual Survey of Manufactures, 33, 49

Brookings Institution: the Nourse project, 37; new index of capacity, 48, 49. *See also* Hickman, Bert

Capacity: diversity of concepts, 28, 29, 30, 31; maximal versus optimal, 31; engineering concept, 36; practical versus rated, 37; formal definition, 47; alternative measures of, 48, 49, 52
Capital-output ratio: use of, in estimating capacity, 34, 35
Census, U.S. Bureau of: capacity project, 48, 49. *See also* Census of Manufactures; Annual Survey of Manufactures
Census of Manufactures, 33
Classification of products: alternative approaches to, 18
Commerce, U.S. Department of. *See* Office of Business Economics (OBE)

Creamer, Daniel. *See* National Industrial Conference Board (NICB)

Deflationary gap, 21
de Leeuw, Frank: on concepts of capacity, 27, 28, 29
Demand: time-distribution of, 37. *See also* Shortrun output-expansion

Federal Reserve Board: alternative weighting schemes, 19; capacity index, 48, 49, 52, 53
Financial variables: significance of, 5, 6, 7, 8, 26
Fortune capacity index, 52

Hickman, Bert: on average cost and capacity, $9n$; on managerial dissatisfaction, 13, 14; involvement with the Brookings Institution capacity index, 48, $49n$, 52

Intermediate products: significance of, 17, 18, 27

Joint costs: allocation of, 8, 17